ĪŚĀ

UPANISHAD

De-gendering Hinduism.

Series Editor: Tapati Bharadwaj.

Published by

LIES AND BIG FEET

ISBN-10: 9384281077

ISBN-13: 978-9384281076

PREFATORY NOTE:

This rendition of an Upanishadic text is but a part of a larger series; the aim of this work is to construe Hindu religious texts as literature, and examine them within a gendered inflected analytical framework. What prevents us from examining the Upanishadic or the Vedic texts within a literary or a gendered perspective? If the basis of religion is "revealed knowledge," which was made evident to men – then is it not obvious that these notions of the Absolute Being would but be defined within gender inflected terminologies? The personal gender-biases of men would affect and predetermine how the notions of the Supreme Being were written about.

Let me explain with an example from an Upanishad. In the Aitareya Upanishad, the first stanza reads in the following manner:

"Om! In the beginning this was but the Absolute Self alone. There was nothing else whatsoever that winked. It thought, 'Let Me create the world.'"

We have to keep in mind that the Vedic texts are partially truthful – they are correct in their explanations on the notion of Absolute Consciousness which becomes matter, and there is no gender ascribed to this Absolute Being. The "Absolute Self" is denoted within gender neutral terms and is referred to as "It."

But there is a slippage which occurs in the Vedic texts, making these texts suspect: it reveals the fact that those who were writing about this kind of revealed, divine knowledge were men and their interests are evident in how the notion of Absolute Consciousness is defined and described. In the same Vedic text, we will find gender specific characteristics of the Absolute Being. The second stanza of the Aitreya Upanishad reads in the following manner:

"He created these worlds, viz. *ambhas*, *marici*, *mara* and *apah*. That which is beyond heaven is *ambhas*. Heaven is its support. The sky is *marici*. The earth is *mara*. The worlds that are below are the *apah*."

A shift occurs whereby, "It" becomes "He": and we all assume, and accept, that the Absolute Being has to be male.

2

To follow this statement to its conclusion, we can state that as the Vedic texts equate the "Absolute Self" with the masculine, men are seen as being agents; in the second part of the Aitreya Upanishad, the first stanza reads: "In man indeed is the soul first conceived"; the implication is that men are agents in determining the birth of children while women are mere passive receptacles.

Biological sciences make use of these dichotomies, and feminists have critiqued how biology (which should be an objective science) makes use of the dominant trope of the "passive" female egg and the "active" male sperm. It is a notion that has also been used since times immemorial in the western worlds, beginning with Aristotle and St. Thomas.

There is no attempt by any religious institution to undress these entrenched misogyny that exists in Hinduism; and these dominant mainstream institutions simply reiterate the status quo. If we pick up a random text on religion that has been published by a well-recognized, religious institution, like the Ramakrishna Mission (that is seen as epitomising modern Hinduism), we find a similar trope operating as the subtext.

In How is a man Reborn, a short text that was published in 1970, by Advaita Ashrama, the publishing house of the Ramakrishna Mission, Swami Satprakashananda makes use of the same above mentioned dichotomy (pp.43-48); he cites instances from the Chandogya Upanishad, the Brhadaranyaka Upanishad, one Dr. Sturtevant, the Aitareya

<u>Upanishad</u> and Sankara to prove the same point, whereby women are seen as passive agents whose only role in society is to procreate while men and sons do all the active work.

We can but make a beginning in dismantling these texts on Hinduism by re-transcribing them. The hope is that our daughters will be able to live in a gender –neutral society.

<u>THE ARRANGEMENT OF THE TEXT</u>:

ON THE LEFT SIDE, THERE IS THE OLDER VERSION OF THE ĪŚĂ UPANISHAD AND THE RIGHT SIDE HAS A REVISED VERSION OF THE TEXT.

ĪŚĂ UPANISHAD

1. *Om.* All this – whatsoever moves on the earth – should be covered by the Lord. Protect (your Self) through that detachment. Do not covet anybody's wealth. (Or – Do not covet, for whose is wealth?)

1. *Om.* All this –
    whatsoever moves on
    the earth – should be
    covered by the
    Supreme Being.
    Protect (your Self)
    through detachment.
    Do not covet
    anybody's wealth. (Or
    – Do not covet, for
    whose is wealth?)

2. By doing *karma,* indeed, should one wish to live here for a hundred years. For a man, such as you (who wants to live thus), there is no way other than this, whereby *karma* may not cling to you.

2. By doing *karma,* indeed, should one wish to live here for a hundred years. For a person, such as you (who wants to live thus), there is no way other than this, whereby *karma* may not cling to you.

3. These worlds of devils
   are covered by
   blinding darkness.
   Those people that kill
   the Self go to them
   after giving up this
   body.

3. These worlds of devils are covered by blinding darkness. Those people that kill the Self go to them after giving up this body.

4. It is unmoving, one, and faster than the mind. The senses could not overtake It, since It had run ahead. Remaining stationary, It outruns all other runners. It being there, Mátariśvā allots (or supports) all activities.

4. It is unmoving, one, and faster than the mind. The senses could not overtake It, since It had run ahead. Remaining stationary, It outruns all other runners. It being there, Mátariśvā allots (or supports) all activities.

5. That moves, That does
not move; That is far
off, That is very near;
That is inside all this,
and That is also
outside all this.

5. That moves, That does not move; That is far off, That is very near; That is inside all this, and That is also outside all this.

6. He who sees all beings
in the Self itself, and
the Self in all beings,
feels no hatred by
virtue of that
(realization).

6. S/he who sees all beings in the Self itself, and the Self in all beings, feels no hatred by virtue of that (realization).

7. When to the man of
    realization all beings
    become the very Self,
    then what delusion
    and what sorrow can
    there be for that seer
    of oneness? (Or – In
    the Self, of the man of
    realization, in which
    all beings become the
    Self, what delusion
    and what sorrow can
    remain for that seer of
    oneness?)

7. When to the person of
   realization all beings
   become the very Self,
   then what delusion
   and what sorrow can
   there be for that seer
   of oneness? (Or – In
   the Self, of the person
   of realization, in which
   all beings become the
   Self, what delusion
   and what sorrow can
   remain for that seer of
   oneness?)

8. He is all-pervasive, pure, bodiless, without wound, without sinews, taintless, untouched by sin, omniscient, ruler of mind, translucent, and self-existent; he has duly allotted the (respective) duties to the eternal years (i.e. to the eternal creators called by that name).

8. S/he is all-pervasive, pure, bodiless, without wound, without sinews, taintless, untouched by sin, omniscient, ruler of mind, translucent, and self-existent; s/he has duly allotted the (respective) duties to the eternal years (i.e. to the eternal creators called by that name).

9. Those that worship *avidya* (rites) enter into blinding darkness; but into greater darkness than that enter they who are engaged in *vidya* (meditation).

9. Those that worship *avidya* (rites) enter into blinding darkness; but into greater darkness than that enter they who are engaged in *vidya* (meditation).

10. "They say that by *vidya* a really different result (is achieved), and they say that by *avidya* a different result is (achieved)", thus have we heard (the teaching) of those wise men who explained that to us.

10. "They say that by *vidya* a really different result (is achieved), and they say that by *avidya* a different result (is achieved)", thus have we heard (the teaching) of those people who explained that to us.

11. He who knows these two, *vidya* and *avidya*, together, attains immortality through *vidya*, by crossing over death through *avidya*.

NEW VERSION OF THE ĪŚĀ UPANISHAD.

11. S/he who knows these two, *vidya* and *avidya*, together, attains immortality through *vidya*, by crossing over death through *avidya*.

12. Those who worship the
Unmanifested
(Prakrti) enter into
blinding darkness; but
those who are devoted
to the Manifested
(Hiranyagarbha) enter
into greater darkness.

12. Those who worship the Unmanifested (Prakrti) enter into blinding darkness; but those who are devoted to the Manifested (Hiranyagarbha) enter into greater darkness.

13. "They spoke of a different result indeed from the worship of the Manifested, and they spoke of a different result from the worship of the Unmanifested" – thus we have heard (the teaching) of those wise men who explained that to us.

13. "They spoke of a different result indeed from the worship of the Manifested, and they spoke of a different result from the worship of the Unmanifested" – thus we have heard (the teaching) of those wise people who explained that to us.

14. He who knows these two, the Unmanifested and the Destruction (Hiranyagarbha), together, attains immortality through the Unmanifested by crossing death through Destruction.

14. S/he who knows these two, the Unmanifested and the Destruction (Hiranyagarbha), together, attains immortality through the Unmanifested by crossing death through Destruction.

15. The face of Truth (Brahman in the solar orb) is concealed by a golden vessel. Do thou, O Sun, open it so as to be seen by me who am by nature truthful (or, am the performer of golden duties).

15. The face of Truth (Brahman in the solar orb) is concealed by a golden vessel. Do thou, O Sun, open it so as to be seen by me who am by nature truthful (or, am the performer of golden duties).

16. O thou who art the nourisher, the solitary traveller, the controller, the acquirer, the son of Prajápati, do remove thy rays, do gather up thy dazzle. I shall behold by thy grace that form of thine which is most benign. I am that very Person that is yonder (in the Sun).

16. O thou who art the nourisher, the solitary traveller, the controller, the acquirer, the child of Prajápati, do remove thy rays, do gather up thy dazzle. I shall behold by thy grace that form of thine which is most benign. I am that very Person that is yonder (in the Sun).

17. Let (my) vital force now attain the (all-pervading) immortal Air; (and) now let this body be reduced to ashes. *Om*, O mind, remember – remember all that has been done. O mind, remember – remember all that has been done.

17. Let (my) vital force now attain the (all-pervading) immortal Air; (and) now let this body be reduced to ashes. *Om*, O mind, remember — remember all that has been done. O mind, remember — remember all that has been done.

18. O Fire! O god! Knowing, as thou do, all our deeds, lead us by the good path for the enjoyment of the fruits of our deeds; remove from us all crooked sins. We offer thee many words of salutation.

18. O Fire! O Divine One!
    Knowing, as thou do, all
    our deeds, lead us by the
    good path for the
    enjoyment of the fruits of
    our deeds; remove from us
    all crooked sins. We offer
    thee many words of
    salutation.

ABOUT THE AUTHOR.

I grew up in an uber-brahmanical family where ritualistic worship was a part of my everyday life; the Vedic texts and the Upanishads were also something I grew up. I always thought that religion was something "out" there; I never actually thought that we were meant to believe in these texts on "revealed knowledge" in an absolute manner. But religion pervades every and all aspects of our lives – institutional, private or public, and be they secular, or not.

After reading the Hindu religious texts for myself, I realised how gendered these texts were, and to our sensibilities, the archaic notions that underlie the basic tenets of Hinduism sound ridiculous and perverse. We forget that the "revealed knowledge" that is evident in the Upanishads has been written by men, and their gender predetermined how they translated the notions of the Absolute Being into language.

I do not want my daughter to grow up within such a flawed belief system; we have to dismantle the existing religious texts as they are and re-transcribe them in order to arrive at gender-neutral concepts of religion, and Being.

www.ingramcontent.com/pod-product-compliance
Lightning Source LLC
Chambersburg PA
CBHW060629030426
42337CB00018B/3275